Creativity Brings Peace

Create & Share Your Gifts

Cheryl Lunar Wind and Friends

Creativity Brings Peace

Create & Share Your Gifts

Some of the poems in this collection first appeared in Follow the White Rabbit, We Are Light and Handshake With the Divine chapbooks; the Lemurian Revival, Spring 2024 and on facebook.

Front cover online.

First edition.

Published by Alexander Agency Books, Mount Shasta, California 96067

ISBN 979-8-9897287-5-6

Creativity Brings Peace

Create & Share Your Gifts

There is no "ownership" here beloved.

All comes from the One Heart space
we all share as expressions of Source.

Masters know this.

Preface

Meliorism--
the belief that we can contribute to positive change
and improve the world through acts of love, creativity,
compassion and kindness.

Follow your heart, your excitement leads the way.
We are here to shine. When we step into our joy
we encourage others to do the same.
Be a beacon.

"As an expression of the Creator you are here to create.

As you create _for you,_ you naturally inspire others.

It is through your expanding joy and passion from within,
by following your excitement and serving all life that the
New Earth creation occurs.

Creativity is God's Function."---Le'Vell Zimmerman

Collaboration is an act of joy through freely sharing
our gifts with others. So much gratitude to the many
open hearted souls who have contributed to these
collections.

"In giving, we receive, in sharing, we find,
A greater purpose, for all mankind.
When self and others, in harmony, blend,
The journey is joyful, right to the end."
---Pradeep Nawarantha

Contents

Creativity
by Le'Vell Zimmerman

Everything you do "matters".

Truly mature souls are never dependent on validation amongst this holographic illusion.

As you create "for you", you naturally inspire others.

This is about expressing yourself, where this is your core purpose of being alive in a physical body beloved.

Seeking approval has always been a form of psychological enslavement.

As an expression of the Creator you are here to create.

This is not only the primary source of your increasing frequency, but also where you are healing the emotional distortions and blockages within your energy centers.

You are here to create the New Earth through your expressions beloved.

Creativity is God's function.

#333

Giving vs Owning
by Cheryl

In the language I was raised with, English---
things are described as in relation to belonging.

This, that----yours, mine.

Very young children are taught---
rights of ownership.

Relationships--
familial and romantic are described this way--
my children, my husband, my partner
My, My, My

Society demands payment for necessities;
such as homes, cars, food, clothes--

Is it any wonder, with receipt in hand,
we say---
my car, my snack, my apartment, my room?

Pets--
my cat, my dog.
Ownership.

My space, my time--leave me alone.

The prophet Gibran states--
'we do not own our children,
they are like arrows shooting
out to space'.

Is this why we are here? to collect
and own as much as possible?

Birds, trees and the earth
give their gifts freely--

Feathers, eggs, leaves, nuts, wood,
rocks, sand, water, ponds, creeks, oceans---

Giving is a gift of free will.

We can give of our time, energy,
compassion, patience and understanding.

The more we give, the more it grows.

The matrix teaches scarcity--
by holding back--
what is rightly for all.

Lets give freely---
Break the program---
Change the language of your thoughts;
and your actions will speak freely---

Giving, Loving and Allowing

"Peace is free, but
Stress costs---
so very much."

The Light at Our Door
by Connie Bonner-Britt, Turtle Woman, Spo- pi- Aakii

New mothers, mothers in delight,
mothers missing their own, yearning a loss beyond words.

Grandmother's heavy load with feelings of sorrow untold.
Mothers gone before us.

Those who are childless,
mothering the ever constant needs of humanity
through birthing yourselves with your timeless gifts.

We are here.

With deep joy for all of our children, each and every one.
We hold heartbreak, unmistakable in its rage.
Yet we hold no regret.

We smile eternal at the memories and blessings
that we hold in our hearts for our dear ones.

We are Mothers holding light for our sacred ones,
wherever they might be...
whether far off and away or traveling with the stars.

We know you, we feel your presence deep and close by,
we listen to your precious messages with our hearts.

Whether close enough to touch and to laugh and hold or at the
distance of a day, our love for our children is never a burden, and
yet we might feel burdened, while in our hearts we are never alone.

We carry you always, even when we know it's time to let you go.

Our children are our wisdom that grows within us each and every
morning; Lifting us, teaching us, honoring us with each step taken
along the way. Each door that's opened, each road traveled, each
heartbreak you hold,
each victory that unfolds...

Our hearts carry abundant joy and love
beyond measure flowing eternal,
an endless treasure.

Go For a Walk
by Le'Vell Zimmerman

When you live more in your own authenticity, you naturally
choose and create paths that stimulate great fulfillment more often.

This graceful state comes with the balance of being
consciously mature enough to sort out and/or take care of
all your conventional responsibilities seamlessly.

It's the expanding capacity of presence you have access to
that allows you to execute when it's time to, versus
carrying around the strain and stress of a mental/emotional
"To-do list", where the emotions of anxiety are clearly draining.

The Heart is truly where the Higher Self lives and is always
capable of doing what needs to be done right now, when it
is presented beyond all anxiety and fear.

It is the voice of the Ego that caters to the idea that "being
concerned" or "worrying all day" is productive, mature, helpful,
or responsible.

It is not.

Often it is more productive to "go for a walk" that to just sit
and worry about something.

Energy flow caters to you accessing solutions from your own inner
genius.

-333

Playground Skills
by Cheryl

What'd ya learn?

I learned that just because
I'm uncomfortable--
Doesn't mean something is
not for me---

Visiting is fun, but
I need my alone time, too!

That good and bad are words
that are restricting.

How we describe a thing
affects the outcome--

When I push out of my
comfort zone--
I create new experiences,

New experiences bring Joy---
+Be In Joy+

Balance is the Key--

Mastering the teeter-totter;
Skills we learned on the playground;

Share with others,
Treat all with kindness and
don't leave anyone hanging.

What did you learn?
by Christine Jamison

I learned a lot about people,
how they act or react to things.

I learned that I can do anything
that I set my mind to.

I learned that people are different,
in all forms.

People act real different when they
are being put on the shelf.

I know that I will learn more as I go
through life,
I'm looking forward to going along
and moving forward.

Make a new start
by Tommy Allen

As the world now seems, to pass me by
Sadly, I can't help, but wonder why

Another sunset I'll never see
Another night I won't be free
Another smile I've missed on your face
Another day here gone to waste
Another sleep dreaming about tomorrow
Another morning waking with sorrow
Another meal surrounded by hate
Another part of me owned by the state
Another fence I can't walk through
Another tear I've shed, with no clue

Then one day, God touches my heart
saying to me, make a new start
be grateful for my gifts, & have some fun
and feel the love, I give everyone
even though life, has you pinned to the wall
learn how to see, the wonder of it all

Another sunrise to share with you
Another daybreak with a new point of view
Another bedtime with prayers to say
Another night to dream this way
Another opportunity to learn something new
Another chance, to write for you
Another meal to feed myself
Another day to better my health
Another day my kids have a dad
Another way for me to be glad
Another love song for us to hear
Another day to love you dear
Another day for a new sensation
Another way to see God's creation

8

I've now learned to be grateful for what I have
And the natural way I make others laugh
God's little gift to see life this way
Each morning I wake is a brand new day
If I begin each morning by reading this poem
Forever in my heart I'll always be home

Mount Lassen
by Tommy Allen

If you climb to the top
  Mount Lassen at nite
  see right straight
to heaven so bright
in this beautiful place
  without a sound
a piece of heaven,
  a treasure found
alone atop this mountain
  God's work of art
as he reached out to me
  touching my heart
I close my eyes
  still see the glow
of the peace & love
  I want to show
asking God
  how can this be
so close to heaven
  can I really see
on this mountain
  secrets found
God's creations
  are all around
we love, we hurt,
  we try and we learn
another page in life
  we now must turn
opening my eyes
  saying goodbye
the shooting star
  that just fell by
the stars one by one
  now fade away
as this mountain of love
  begins a new day
another precious gift
  one more sunrise
to be cherished forever
10

hiding my cries
As this night now ends
what do I find
this mountain of love
all on my mind
Its time to walk
home to bed
I'll never forget
what, to me, God said
Treasure all the secrets
you learned up here
and for you this mountain
will always be near

Simple Acts
by Pradeep Nawarathna

In the garden of life, where dreams take flight,
Happiness blossoms, in the day and night.
When work is joy, and words are kind,
A symphony of peace, in heart and mind.

For every deed that lifts anothers load,
Plants a seed of joy, along the road.
And every word that heals a heart in pain,
Is like a gentle rain, on a parched plain.

In giving, we receive, in sharing, we find,
A greater purpose, for all mankind.
When self and others, in harmony, blend,
The journey is joyful, right to the end.

So let your work be love, made visible,
And your words, a balm, so invincible.
For happiness comes, not in gold or fame,
But in simple acts, that kindle a flame.

A flame of hope, in a world so wide,
Where the light of joy, can't be denied.
For when we serve, with a willing heart,
Happiness comes, and never shall part.

Purity
by Pradeep Nawarathna

A mind serene, a heart so light,
Free from the shadows of the night.
Attachments fall, like leaves in breeze,
Inner peace found, with graceful ease.

Conduct kind, with compassion's guide,
Harmonious bonds, in trust abide.
Purity's seed, in thought and deed,
Blooms a garden, free from greed.

Refrain from harm, let virtues grow,
Integrity's stream, in sunlight's glow.
Authentic paths, with purpose tread,
Life's tapestry, with joy is spread.

Mindful steps, with ethics sure,
Resilience forged, to endure.
Grace in trials, strength within,
Equanimity's calm, amidst life's din.

Interconnected, all life's throng,
In joy's chorus, we belong.
Welfare's gift, to others lend,
Fulfillment's journey, without end.

Pursue the pure, in mind and act,
A life of meaning, in fact.
Happiness true, contentment's start,
In the simple poem, of the heart.

Old Man
by Akaya Rose

Old Man,
I look at you and remember long ago
I loved you so much then
Your crystal mind, your body, strong
Your movements deliberate, lithe,
like the walk of a lion
Pacing over the rise of a mountain
Your laughter sweet and sudden
And your voice deep and liquid
Like slow moving rivers
I was your sweetheart, your lover.

I watched you walk softly, firmly
Across bridges filled with danger
Clear eyes quiet and penetrating
Quiet compassion etching your face
While strong hands were always
busy fixing something
Shoulders straining to lift other's heavy burdens,
from weight crushing the
fragile strands of hope,
Still remaining.
I will be yours forever.

Today, I see your hands
old and rippled, like the ocean
in the wake of a storm.
Bones creaking like an old rocking chair.
Molded by many weights and shapes
Roughed and carved by winds of change
And the needs of the day
Voices always demanding more from you
Over the years,
and when I remember the soft sounds
Deep in the night, of hands patting so gently
To sooth our babies cries
Or your touch so sweet on my body,
Waterfalls of feeling course through me
I was your wife.

I see your long arms tired,
legs aching,
Lower back sore when you moved
And I am here beside you in the morning
When you got up slowly,
Carefully, just as you do now,
I lay here quietly
in awe of your lion's heart
Rising up again
defying your body's pain.
Thinking, how could I have been so lucky
as to be with you.

I know you loved me
by Akaya Rose

Then my night storm cried in the turbulence
from life's fractured mirrors making non-sense
sketches of stories flashed through my life
across a widening ravine interrupted by strife
like fiction you'd see on a movie screen
smoke hiding your real world from being seen

I thank you for loving me anyway
trying to protect me so I would stay.

While lies spun together twisted like twine
Rolling off tongues sputtering with wine
seeing dark eyes once beautiful, veiled in pain
broad shoulders braced against deepening shame
Face turned away from the motionless knowing,
My shadowed wind-blown heart blowing

And you loved me enough though,
didn't you...
to distance the smoke fumes, the bubbling brew
so I could believe in what you wanted to be,
my untarnished image never let you feel free.

I could have loved you forever you know
But loving a mirage means you have to let go

Lightning
by Akaya Rose

Have
you ever dreamed of being
A lightning rod
upon tomorrow's roof
drawing unearthly power from
beneath heaven's door
to strike the heart of a woman
such as me

I have dreamed
Of being struck by rainstorms
of light, riding
sounds of Thunder
rocking my waters like endless seas
Stirring eons of feelings so softly

Shivering
You feel the breeze
Like an almost perceptible
Breath of love upon you

Sirens
by Akaya Rose

No sirens were heard in the painful night
Just speechless words in the dusty light

No sirens were heard when the day came
The heart knew it was lies to blame

A woman cannot stay with a man like this
Lips that lie even while they kiss

And I thought you knew a higher way
I was wrong to believe, wrong to stay

Appreciate Life
by Mary Schrack

Life is unfair when your poor---
but, really

Family is Life.

Happiness comes from within---
not earned.

We live within our means--
Stand Proud,
we made it to retirement.

Only now, do we
Learn
to Appreciate Life.

Rinse and Repeat
by David Kolden

What'd ya learn?

"The golden rule."

Not that golden rule,
the other one.

"Those with all the gold rule."

They make laws that help them acquire more gold--
They understand well that wealth is a function of power,
and power is the means of acquiring more wealth;

Rinse and Repeat--
Endless Cycle.

How Do We Get Out?
by Cheryl

We get out of the Rinse & Repeat Cycle--
by not playing.

Just don't play the game.

We do what Mary said--
"Appreciate Life."

Live within our means--

It's the little things that count.

Wisdom of Pain
by Mercy Talley

And there is the
Lifting Up
The Opening unto
The Dawn
As the first morning
Fresh & Unencumbered
Though Deepened with
Wisdom
The sharpness of Pain
Woven
In the wake
Of Heart Knowing
Touched by Breath
In the Tapestry of Being
~

Peace Speaks Truth
by Mercy Talley

My Spirit floats to a
farther shore where
Peace speaks Truth
& Sorrow is no more

No longer tethered
to confusion & division
Humanity gathers in
Unity & Inclusion

Heart to Heart
Soul to Soul
Reach out to See
Love brings Clarity

Equanimity
by Pradeep Nawarathna

With a heart unmoved by the ebb and flow,
In the face of life's high and low,
Equanimity is the tranquil tide,
Where calm reason and happiness reside.

It's the steady hand in a stormy sea,
The quiet resolve to let life be.
A balanced stance in the dance of fate,
Where inner joy does not abate.

In equanimity, find strength to cope,
With every challenge, with every hope.
For in the center of life's great swirl,
Lies the pearl of peace, unswirled.

My Weapon (from Iraq)
by Devon Hansen

Oh, how my hands remember you, and feel you,
and know your every detail. How my thumb will
never forget the feel of pushing off your safety.
How my finger feels on your trigger.

And, how my very core has felt a darkness
towards you. How my eyes seemingly see
a dark world when I think of you. For so many
years you've been this ominous being always
with me in some bizarre spirit. Heavy and
reeking of the scent of oil and gun powder.
I hated you.

Yet you were there for me when I needed you
most. I'm alive because of you. Yet you've
hurt people, yet your innocent. You didn't
ask to be in a war, nor did you ask to be a
weapon, you were innocent, as the soldiers
and marines, and other combatants who
were born as babies into the world.

You are elements of the earth taken and
forged into a weapon against your will.
You could have been forged into a musical
instrument, a garden tool, or anything else
to enrich others or left as part of the earth.

You've served a long and hard life surrounded
by death, even helping to create it, and you've
never had any choice in it. I want to thank you
and forgive you, and hope wherever you are
your life is no longer a weapon.

Streets of Hell (Battle of Fallujah)
by Devon Hansen

20 years ago
8000 miles away
Still tortured to this day
As if it was yesterday
Streets of war
Streets of hell
My mind forever trapped in war
Unimaginable streets of killing
Darkness comes
Only sleepless nights come
Terror comes in waking nightmares
Is this punishment and torture from
the universe?
Pain and despair
Can my body ever be repaired?
Lonely, yet united in our torture
High spirits unite us in our pride
We'd do it all again
Misery in battle
Bonded in our trauma
Hell to never be understood
Is Hell waiting for us in the next life?
For now I shall learn to live my life

"For those of us who as young men and women that truly fought in combat upholding a calling greater than ourselves, we'll forever be in the search of healing and for moments of peace, and they'll always be worth the search, however long it may be".

Bees are Free
by Cody Ray Richardson

When I was a child
I would catch bees
I would hold them in my hand
I would then count to ten

If they did not stung me
I would let them go
I loved letting them go
I felt bad when they were bad

Go free I would say
You have passed the test of patients
You are a gentle creature
Go on with your life

If they were to sting me
I would eat them
You were not patient my friend
You are a mean bee

I was only testing you
To see if you were safe
For the sake of my sisters and brothers
The garden must bee safe from stings

Now I am grown I see the truth
I was the one who grabbed them
Now I see the culprit was me
I leave the bees to be free

God was a child long before he was a god

Pure Reflection
by Cody Ray Richardson

Can we see a stranger as a friend
Will we trade the future for the past again
Do we see each other or only see them
Reality or projection
Closed off
Or open
The ones that hurt us
The ones that helped us heal
Ones that shut us down
Ones that helped us feel
Who are we to know who is who
This endless game of chance
Will we stay curled up in a ball
Or will we dance
In the sun
Deep in sweet spring waters
I see my reflection
I am still pure as this connection
You look the same to me
I mean to leave you as you are found
No past
No future
Pure as water
Though it goes deep in its depths
Water can never drown

Be You
by Lauren Willow Fox

You
A divine soul
Remember
Renew
Rejoice!
To hear
Your voice
A choice
To live
To love
To laugh
Identity
Strong
Nobody
Wrong
Or right
No fight
Ego death
Reach to sky
Touch the earth
Smile
Compost old
Stories told
Past healed
Find your way
Present day
Show your face
Share
Embrace
Sun Dance
Rain dance
Earth dance
Be danced
Be loved
Be You

The Vision
by Wesley Buniger

As a vision, it came to me a year ago, shortly after moving to
Mount Shasta.
The work I see before me is none other than a labor of love.
It involves helping others get in touch with themselves by
way of working with their hands.
I entertained the idea, but tried to lose it in other activities,
but still the feeling remained...

So here it is---
People continue to come to me saying they appreciate that which
I create, always, they are surprised at the diversity of what I
produce.
But, unable to understand how I do it.
To me, it is my breath.
I have meditated by doing for so long, it has become a way of being.

The vision is to impart this ability to others so that they of their own
nature and at their own pace become aware of being completely
themselves.
This is accomplished by awakening to one's own intuition
and the use of common sense.
Common sense is the field where spontaneity finds its spark.
It is that place, where according to ones own personal clarity---

Authenticity finds its source.

ZERO
by Guthema Roba

Why afraid of being
nobody or nothing?
nothingness is infinite
possibility.
It is ultimate bliss,
the beginning of
everything.
Remember that the
most graceful number
in mathematics is zero.
It is graceful because
It is a silent state.
It is a field of awareness.
It is only when we are empty,
grace descends on us.
Everything comes spinning
out of nothingness
and eventually returns
to nothingness.
In the end we all
have to rest.
We are destined to
come home.

Shine Brighter
By Le'Vell Zimmerman

Don't let anyone "dim" your Light beloved.

It's always necessary to shine brighter.

This is not about you "getting away from" or avoiding anyone in your experience.

This is about you having the strength and maturity to accept everyone, while making your own decisions about where you invest your time and energy.

Your brilliance is healing amongst all Life.

-333

Love Is Not Logical
by Le'Vell Zimmerman

No,
your healing path will not "make sense",
where Love is not "logical" beloved.

Infinite Intelligence remains beyond all logical
comprehension.

This experience is your own design,
where it is only necessary to trust yourself
and make decisions using your own intuition
as an internal guidance system.

Do you trust yourself beloved?

A Response
by A'Marie B. Thomas-Brown

Waking up from a long sleep
The wind
The whales
The birds
The trees
Such glee as I am remembering
Your laughter and humor
To be awakened from slumbering stupor
To see what living is for
Hiding the light no more
As ignorance is not bliss
I stand face to face
And we kiss
Love intertwines in the words, the spaces,
the diction
As we listen to the sound
As Light
We ride
The tide
Ocean to Ocean
Moment by Moment
Beyond breath
With nothing left I wept

May Love Lead
Spirit keep
And we breathe
As One

Painted Feelings
by Tommy Allen

A Flowing river
  in the mountain air
I see the girl
  I see her stare

painting on a rock
  'now please be still'
is all that she says
  up on that hill

I don't understand
  what's inside of me
she asks in thoughts
  'let me see'

all your love
  emotions inside
allow me to feel
  what's in your mind

share these things
  and open your heart
so I can finish this painting
  my work of art

I open my heart
  at her request
sharing these things
  laying to rest

A peaceful feeling
  like never before
fills me with love
  and so much more

she smiles at me
  as she strokes her brush
the river rolls by
  in no rush

32

smiling now
  blowing in the breeze
as she views her painting
  down on her knees

she invites me over
  gives me a clue
prepare for this
  what I see in you

I look at the painting
  and what do I see
she painted all the feelings
  inside of me

Universal Creed
by Pradeep Nawarathna

Kindness, a light that guides the way,
In every act, in what we say.
Compassion, a path that's true and tried,
In giving, we receive, side by side.

No faith owns the gentle deed,
It's the *universal creed* we need.
A smile, a hand, a heart that sees,
In kindness, we find our peace.

Small acts, like seeds, we scatter wide,
In love's rich soil, they'll abide.
Forgive, embrace, let go of fear,
In compassion's glow, we draw near.

So let us live with open hands,
And love that understands.
For kindness is the purest art,
The song of the compassionate heart.

Princes and Kings
by Tommy Allen

Let me tell you
 about Princes and Kings
traveling thru time
 searching for gold dust rings

they sprinkle their gold,
 on broken hearts
granting a wish,
 a brand new start

the gold dust lights up
 our darkest nites
glitters of love,
 oh so bright

A lonely heart,
 needs gold dust rings
as they offer this gift,
 wrapped in strings

these Princes and Kings,
 are everywhere you go
setting up these rings,
 watching them grow

their works not done,
 until i see
all the gold dust rings,
 inside of me

these gold dust rings,
 I put in my rhyme
Will watch over your heart,
 every time

what makes them so precious,
 priceless & true
these Princes and Kings,
 live inside of you

Spirit of America
by Alyssa Narum

A voice she called me gently in the stillness of my mind

She told me of a beauty way an open heart can find

I asked her who she was and she answered clear and true

Twas the Spirit of America

She led me through her mountains and her prosperous golden fields

And showed me what a abundance a fertile love can yield

So I thank the lord above for this opportunity

With the Spirit of America

Spirit of America
Sacred wisdom in her breeze
Teachers made of animal
And temples made of tree

Ancestors that are dwelling in her valleys and her streams

Protect her for her children so they can fulfill their dreams

So I lift my heart in reverence to the first peoples still entwined

Within the Spirit of America

Grandfather and grandmother in ceremony

Breathed into her a vision of peace and harmony

So we come together of different color to create a world anew

Upon the Spirit of America

Spirit of America
Sacred wisdom in her breeze
Teachers made of animal
And temples made of tree

Hey yanna hey yanna ho hey yanna ho.
Hey ney oh wey. Hey ney oh wey. Hey ney oh wey.

From the Amazonian jungle to the Yukon of white snow

Her loving guidance shows me what a human mind can't know

So I give myself in service to that guide that came to me

As the Spirit of America

She asks us all to rise up in this never-ending hymn

To learn how to treat her by looking from within

So we'll walk this path of beauty, hand in hand we go

Upon the Spirit of America

Spirit of America
Sacred wisdom in her breeze
Teachers made of animal
And temples made of tree

Hey yanna hey yanna ho hey yanna ho.
Hey ney oh wey. Hey ney oh wey. Hey ney oh wey.

Oil & Water
by Cheryl

Imagine a reality where the trees talk to you---
The giving tree---
Its said "You get what you give".

A New world---
where all is shared---afterall,
everything we have is a gift from the universe.

My learning will be
primal, natural, eternal.
The forest is my guru.

Look to the elders---
they carry wisdom bundles---
like a cord of wood--
Do they charge a special price---
$144 for a bundle?

The teachings are clear--
like water--
The cost or fee is like oil---
not clean.
Clouds up the clear.
Oil and water don't mix.

Church and State.
Step away from the matrix.

The sacred way has all but become polluted with commerce---
It is not needed.
There is another way.

Physical cost is for physical things.
Sacred things are a gift.

Ask your ancestors---
talk to the masters--
how to move into the new
5D Earth?

Live a new way
by
remembering the old ways.

Let go of the belief--
there must be a gift for a gift--
Become light as a feather
in your giving.
The exchange will be your freedom.

What holds you back keeps
this reality in place.
What are you holding onto?

The indigenous know
not to charge
for what is sacred.

Our ancestors are waiting for us---
give up the bone.

Be open to new ways
of doing, thinking, and living.
Ask yourself--
What is the next best step?
Do that.
Step by step--
we gain our
freedom and victory!

The New Earth
by Le'Vell Zimmerman

Only when you focus your aim do you
"spark a flame".

Here is where you realize that to be more present
is to "set yourself on fire".

Be still,
then create beloved.

It is through your expanding joy and passion from within,
by following your excitement and serving all life that
"The New Earth" creation occurs.

We ground ourselves through stillness when we
wake up and get to work.

It's a great honor to serve all life throughout
The Multiverse.

Salute the Fleet.

#333

Many thanks to these contributors:

Tommy Allen

Connie Bonner-Britt, Turtle Woman, Spo- pi- Aakii

Wesley Buniger

A'Marie B. Thomas-Brown

Lauren Willow Fox

Devon Hansen

Christine Jamison

David Kolden

Alyssa Narum

Pradeep Nawarathna

Cody Ray Richardson

Guthema Roba

Akaya Rose

Mary Schrack

Mercy Talley

Le'Vell Zimmerman

Author page--

Cheryl Lunar Wind lives in the Mount Shasta area in a little town called Weed. She is a practicer of Mayan cosmology, Lakota ceremony, Star Knowledge and the Universal Laws including the Law of One. Her hobbies are writing poetry, music, dance, drum circles and love for all life; plant, animal and crystal. Cheryl has been a guide and spiritual teacher for many years. Now she shares wit and wisdom through poetry, and has published poetry books; Know Your Way, We Are One, Follow the White Rabbit, Love Your Light, LIFE: Shared thru Poetry, Come to Mount Shasta: Sacred Path Poetry, We Are Light, Finding Our Way Home, We Are Forever, Handshake With the Divine, Grand Rising: A New Day Has Dawned, Star Messages: Codes to Sing, Dance and Live by, Return to Innocence, Bloom Like Nature: Live the Natural Way and Creativity Brings Peace: Create & Share Your Gifts.

Testimonials---

"Cheryl's poetry is very inspiring--particularly the way she compares life with the forces of nature. There is a special element in her poems that opens my heart and fills my soul with divine possibilities."
Giovanna Taormina, Co-Founder, One Circle Foundation

"Cheryl's poems have helped me to uncover and honor my own hidden memories. The beauty of her spirit is evident in each tender, insightful passage."
Marguerite Lorimer, www.earthalive.com

"A rare collection filled with raw, courageous honesty. Thought provoking words that will stop you in your tracks."
Snow Thorner, ED Open Sky Gallery, Montague, California

"When wisdom, guidance, confirming comfort, ect. arrives to us humans--from beings with the perspective of other realms--it is a divine gift. Especially in the form of what we call poetry, and through a being with no agenda; Cheryl Lunar Wind simply shares what source gives her!"---Dragon Love (Thomas) Budde

Cheryl,
Greetings and Happy Monday to you my friend. I just
wanted to share with you that every time I read
'Come to Mount Shasta', even now that I'm mentioning
it I cry, I cannot help it, it is such a Divine message and
so impeccable in its timing. I came up here for Spirit, you
know I was called by Source and I live on the mountain
and I just want to thank you. Your poem found me last
summer at the headwaters during the Alien and Angels
conference; and then I found your book sitting in the
gazebo and I just can't stop, I love it! I love you, thank you.
---Jim

Cheryl,
Just want to thank you for your bringing me into the community
at Shasta. What you are doing/did do is absolutely changing
my life. You did it, you were instrumental in helping me set
my true path. Spirit is moving and the more of us that listen
and act the sooner the shift will be completed.
---Darrel

About Cheryl's poetry--
"You are dynamic! I have known no one who does so much so
swiftly, and your writing touches my heart because it comes
from your heart."
---The Durwood Show

"Your words are my words. I keep your book 'Know Your Way'
on my nightstand. I read it at bedtime and morning."
---Karina Arroyo

"Cheryl's words work magic in my heart, stirring the wisdom
that is buried so deeply within me---beautiful indeed!"
---Ellie Pfeiffer, founder of Ellie's Espresso & Bakery, Weed, CA